The Nightmare
of
Hillsborough

Mike Bartram

First Published 2011 by Countyvise Ltd
14 Appin Road, Birkenhead, CH41 9HH

Copyright © 2011 Mike Bartram

The right of Mike Bartram to be identified as the author of this work has been asserted by him in accordance with the Copyright, Design and Patents Act 1988.

British Library Cataloguing in Publication Data.
A catalogue record for this book is available from the British Library.

ISBN 978 1 906823 50 4

This book is dedicated to the 96 people
who lost their lives at Hillsborough
&
to all those 'Victims Without A Number'

This book contains several poems relating to Post Traumatic
Stress Disorder (PTSD). If you think you, or anybody you
know may be suffering from this condition and feel the need
for advice or help please contact the Registered Mental
Health Charity Imagine:
www.imaginementalhealth.org.uk

The Nightmare of Hillsborough

Contents

Foreword

Mike approached me at a Hillsborough Justice Campaign event that my Mum and I had arranged for my Dad's 50th birthday. He had heard Dad's story and after realising that there are "innocent victims without a number, and to the world they remain largely unknown" he had written a poem called 'Victim's without a number'.

The poem highlights that there are still people suffering from the disaster and the number will keep on growing. This was an overwhelming gesture that was appreciated by the whole family. So when Mike approached me for a second time, asking me to write this foreword for his new book of poetry, this would start with the poem inspired by Dad's story, I was honoured.

I am the daughter of a huge LFC fan, season ticket holder until 15th April 1989, a victim of the Hillsborough disaster. Dad didn't die on that day; he was there, he felt the panic, suffered the pain, the anxiety and the tragic loss of his friend and fellow psychiatric nurse; one of the unfortunate 96. From that day my Dad, Ronnie King, suffered with post traumatic stress disorder (PTSD). Nightmares, guilt and a fear of crowded places, he never went to a match again. My younger brother and sister never got to go to a football game with him, which was a great sadness since he had always envisaged us all being season ticket holders. After much torment and in the wake of Kelvin Mackenzie's appearance on Newsnight, he ended his own life in 2007.

The Hillsborough Justice Campaign and Peter Carney from the families group have supported my Mum, brother, sister and me through the difficult times and continue to offer support, they will never know how much this means to us and no doubt to other families who have suffered due to that awful day. 'The Nightmare of Hillsborough' is a creative way of getting across the message that "96 is not set in stone" (Victim's Without A Number) and many others are still suffering.

Mike Bartram's distinctive style of not holding back and saying it how it is, emphasises not only his opinion but just how much we are all still fighting for what's right. The story of the 'Hillsborough Disaster' lives on through generations. I am one of the growing numbers that has suffered and will continue to suffer as a result of that day but will not let it be forgotten. The anger towards various authorities is shown in our voices and text, as we relive the day that caused heartache to so many, and will continue to do so. The theme that runs through everything related to the Hillsborough disaster and that Mike calls attention to in all of his poetry (In '20 Years On' and 'Justice Call', as well as this book) is that we will not stop fighting until we get JUSTICE and THE TRUTH.

Rachel King

Ronnie King (with birthday cake!)

Victims Without A Number

They talk about the Hillsborough victims in numbers, '96' is what they always quote.
That's the figure it says on all the banners, and all the poems that I've ever wrote.
At the anniversary service each year, 96 is the amount of candles that they light.
And it's on behalf of 'the 96,' that we continue our Hillsborough Justice Campaign fight.
There are 96 names written on the memorials, and its 96 names each year that are read out loud.
We say a little prayer for each and every one of them, as our heads are all bowed.
But there have been more victims of Hillsborough over the years, so that number 96 is not set in stone.
These are the innocent victims without a number, and to the world they remain largely unknown.
I've just sadly heard of another loss of life due to Hillsborough, so the number of victims still grows.
So at the memorial service next year at Anfield I will say an extra prayer, and I will carry an extra rose.

Spring

I heard a couple of sad stories recently, as spring looks like it's finally on the way.
But spring is a season I don't like, if nature could only keep those flowers at bay.
I heard a couple of sad stories recently, as daffodils all start to bloom across the land.
But early spring is a season I don't like, especially on days when the sun has got the upper hand.

I thought I'd heard most of the sad stories about Hillsborough, but today I heard one that was new.
It involved a so called 'impartial' Police Force that was clearly protecting its mates in blue.
I was told about insensitive coppers and about the wrong information sadly sent out to one man.
I heard that these officers never even apologized, never mind having to carry the can.

It's been a long, cold winter this year; we've had ice and plenty of snow that was deep.
But spring is about to take over, because after all nature does have a promise to keep.
The lakes will all be flowing again, no longer buried under a thick ice that wouldn't crack.
But when early spring arrives I just sometimes feel only sorrow, not the warm sun on my back.

Everyday

Everyday is a sad one, to some extent or to some degree.
There's always something to remind me, always something to make me see.
Every time there's a match on, something doesn't seem quite right.
Sometimes I even feel a little guilty, when I should only feel delight.
Everyday is a new one; of course we all know that to be true.
But some things just won't go away, do you ever get that feeling too?
Tomorrow is another day, but everyday seems to be the same.
At some stage during that day, I'm bound to feel a little pain.

Selective/Defective

Pick a line here, pick a snippet there, and cut a sentence or two a little short.
Piece it all together and make it say what you want, had to be your only thought.
Dismiss the bigger picture, and gloss over all the words that prove you wrong.
Ignore the clear evidence put before you, so you can make your viewpoint strong.
Choose a paragraph, any paragraph, but carefully only quote the bits that you need.
Paste and glue all your 'evidence' and 'findings' together, just so you can plant a seed.
But don't take the world for fools Mr Hawker; it's clear to see you don't have a case.
You should have backed down from the start, but you lack dignity, honour and grace.
You seem determined to hide from the truth Mr Hawker why can that possibly be?
The truth puts paid to your every argument, and that's plain for the world to see.

Pass It On

Make sure that you pass the story on, hand it down from parent to daughter or son.
Tell your children the tale of Hillsborough, and tell them what still needs to be done.
Tell them about all those heroes, heroes that made you proud to be a red.
Heroes then disgracefully accused of robbing from the injured and the dead.

When your children are older, or when you think that the time is about right.
Tell them the truth about Hillsborough and tell them all about our plight.
Explain to them about truth and justice, and about the ongoing campaigns.
And when you find the right moment maybe read out all 96 names.

Pass it on all about The Sun newspaper, and why in Liverpool it still fails to sell.
Pass it on all about Kelvin MacKenzie, an editor that chose only filthy lies to tell.
And when you talk to your children about Hillsborough, don't ever be afraid to cry.
And as every one of your tear drops fall, each one can have its own reason why.

Pass it on also about those who have stood in our corner, and faced the authorities toe to toe.
These people who have fought for and demanded answers, the sort of people that will never let go.
So tell all this to your kids as they get older, and when they take up the beautiful game.
And when they're old enough to understand, stress the significance of that flame.

Bridges

Although your defence was paper thin and our case was
watertight.
So where did it all go wrong and now why this long a fight?
A justice system famed for its honesty, and renowned for its
British sense of fair play.
But somehow justice for the 96 went right out of the window
that day.
Those 21 years of injustice have gone now; I suppose
they've gone for good.
But you can still put things right, if you have a conscience
then you know you should.
Let's now build bridges of iron and pull down those weak
old bridges of rope.
As the family and friends of the 96 now deserve to have
some faith, some belief and some hope.

Hillsborough (The Stadium)

Built in 1899, Hillsborough went on to be one of the finest stadiums of its time.
I always remember the old Kop; it looked like a wild hill eating into the skyline.
The famous North Stand opened in 1961, still looks fantastic to this very day.
A structure that was a remarkable achievement back then, and has stood the test of time in every way.

They put a roof on their Kop in 86,' and levelled out that irregular shaped bank.
And although the new Kop looked impressive, the ground seemed to lose the oddity in its rank.
The old South Stand was mostly rebuilt, but still oozed Leitch's style and grace.
The roof gable was replicated and restored, centred by that famous clock face.

The 'Leppings Lane' doesn't exist now as a terrace, it's just part of the West Stand, disguised in seats of blue.
After 'Hillsborough' that end should have been demolished, is some people's point of view.
They have some grand plans for Hillsborough, as the crown it once wore couldn't last.
But sadly for some Hillsborough stadium, will always be haunted by the ghosts of its past.

Altered Police Statements

'Do you ever want promotion?' joked a police typist, she
said this to a junior cop.
He had just handed in his Hillsborough statement; it was
how he saw it, nothing over the top.
His notes just stated facts, and what he witnessed he
wanted to truthfully report.
But parts of his statement annoyed the censor, as they
would not look too good in Court.

'Utter confusion' was altered in one PC's statement, to read
instead 'confusion reigned'
It was deemed an 'adverse comment' when an officer said
that due to lack of Police control he 'felt ashamed'.
It was mentioned in statements the concern of lack of radios
and of insufficient command.
But the typed up versions of these notes, did not always
match what was written by hand.

Lawyers estimate 183 PC statements were edited to suit the
South Yorkshire's Police Forces need.
And when asked to countersign these altered statements
not all of the police officers agreed.
But alterations were made nevertheless, and some
statements came in versions 1, 2 and 3.
A statement though about fans climbing walls to get in was
marked as 'OK. Good statement for the SYP'

Owls and Blades

A city with 2 major football teams, one in stripes of blue the other in stripes of red.

And in that Sheffield City all those years ago many of our tears were sadly shed.

A city where so many lives were needlessly lost, that doesn't seem right or fair.

Hearts shouldn't be broken at a football match, not when broken beyond repair.

21 years later, I hope all the Wednesday and United fans understand how we still feel.

How we're still searching for all the answers, because the truth they've still yet to reveal.

'Hillsborough' could have claimed the lives of any football fans, could have easily been that of an 'owl' or a 'blade'.

So please support us in our fight for justice, and never let your memories of the 96 ever fade.

Gutter Press

Why did you have to hurt our city? a city already down on its knees in pain.
Did you have to blacken our reputation, which to this day still bares the stain?
Did you have to put the knife in, and then did you have to twist the blade?
Did you not have any feelings for those families, while the flowers were still being laid?
Gutter Press is what you're labelled, and that's what you are, gutter press.
You told all those lies about our supporters, you caused nothing but distress.
They say that the truth can hurt sometimes, but I tell you lies can hurt even more.
And the lies you told still hurt today, you're just gutter press and rotten to the core.

Will You Be There?

Will you be there again this year, will you be at Anfield to take your seat?
Will you be there again this year, to say some prayers while on your feet?
Will you be there again this year, to witness there's a battle for justice still to be fought?
Or was last year's visit a one off, just a Hillsborough 20th anniversary to report?

Will you be there again this year, to see racks of candles and 96 burning flames?
Will you be there again this year, to see the tears as they read out all 96 names?
I take it you were there last year, when those 96 red balloons were all freed?
But will you be at Anfield again this year, or don't you think there's the need?

Last year 'Hillsborough' was 'good copy' it felt like the whole world wanted to know.
And last year's turnout was fantastic, as we watched the massive crowd grow and grow.
But what will it be like this year; will the media descend on Anfield once more?
As shouldn't they be there every year, because that's what anniversaries are for.

Roll up....Roll up

Roll up, roll up, come on and see the show.
This should be a one off event, but you never know.
Roll up, roll up, come and hear some lies.
Justice or freedom up for grabs as a prize.

Roll up, roll up, and watch this whitewash unfold.
And spot the secret handshakes as those lies are told.
Roll up, roll up, a miscarriage of justice on the way.
96 innocent people dead but will anyone have to pay?

Roll up, roll up, and see how low some people will sink.
Hear them blame the fans, hear them blame the drink.
Roll up, roll up, this should be an open and shut case.
We know who was to blame, but what punishment would
they face?

Roll up, roll up, it's soon time for the final act.
A decision soon to be made though will it be based on fact?
Roll up, roll up, and you won't be sorry if you come.
Don't miss this farce of the century, don't miss the judge
have his fun.

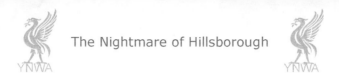
Villa Park Announcement

'The Liverpool game has been abandoned' it was announced at Villa Park.
Nobody really knew why that was, both sets of fans remained in the dark.
But when that game was over, people gathered around car radios for news.
Everton had just reached Wembley, but there was no celebrating from the blues.
As one Evertonian said they were drinking beer, but that beer had no taste.
His mind was only fixed on Hillsborough, and the shock of that tragic waste.
The Cup Final didn't seem important anymore, going to Wembley no big deal.
People had lost their taste for football; the Twin Towers had lost their appeal.

A Long Time

It's been such a long time now since you did us so much wrong.
I've been so proud of our strength in that time, we've always stood tall and strong.
It's been such a long time now, since you sent all that pain our way.
Why don't you just tell us the truth, please tell me why the delay?
You're talking to us now and about some things we may now agree.
You should have listened earlier though about that 'cut off' time of quarter past three.
How much suffering could you have saved people if you were more open years ago?
And I'm still waiting for the guilty parties for some genuine remorse to show.
Hopefully after the year 2012, we'll have no need to campaign or to fight anymore.
Unless that is you have more delaying tactics in place, or more dirty tricks in store.

That Kennedy Moment

21 years ago to this very day I took part in a football game.
It was a Zingari Amateur football match; Liobians was my team's name.
We kicked off that match at about 2 o'clock, half time came at about quarter to 3.
Half of us didn't even want to play, because we thought Hillsborough was the place to be.

So when our half time arrived, and because our side was full of ardent reds and blues.
We all gathered around a small radio set to listen to the latest semi final news.
But soon our game kicked off again, and ended at about twenty to 4.
And the first thing we did then of course was to find out on that radio the latest FA Cup score.

But we were told that Liverpool's match had been abandoned, though details were vague and scarce.
We didn't realise at that time that things were going to get much worse.
I went straight home from our match to switch on the radio and television set.
And soon I realised that a day to remember for so many had sadly turned into a day to regret.

The gravity of the tragedy unfolded 'live' as worried loved ones all reached for their phones.
Words were spoken softly by all the reporters in sombre and mournful tones.
Emergency telephone numbers for people to call were left permanently on our television screens.
That dreadful day that so many lives were destroyed along with so many hopes and dreams.

'Invisible' Illness

Some people have what you could call an 'Invisible Illness'
they innocently caught it at a football match.
They have no broken bones to repair, no visible scars to
heal, not even a tiny cut or a scratch.
But what they do have is a broken mind, and that can be
harder to mend than any shattered bone.
These people with an invisible illness went to Hillsborough
a very different person from the one that eventually came
home.
An invisible illness can be a well kept secret, an inner
torment that a person may choose to fight on their own two
feet.
Such people may be afraid to share their feelings, if so their
illness becomes almost impossible to spot or to treat.
I often wonder what kind struggle it must be for a person to
suffer alone, wrapped inside an invisible chain.
But if the world showed more compassion and
understanding towards mental illness, maybe the stigma
would no longer remain.

The Banner

A famous banner lies stretched out, covering part of a car park floor.
People stand all around it, and admire what that banner stands for.
The sun produces a shaft of light which arrows down a hazy beam.
It falls on this Justice banner, of Celtic colours, yellow and green.
A banner which lies flat on the ground, proudly displayed for all to see.
The banner carries a message of unity, and that's so important to me.
And the sun spared a dagger of light, to shine on this banner that day.
The banner and sky became one, connected strangely with that ray.
A banner that brings two sides together, with passion, pride and fight.
And maybe God looked upon it that day, and blessed it with his light.

What Kind Of Country

Just what kind of country do we live in, honestly where is it really at?

Why should we have to fight for justice, I've never been able to understand that.

I mean, why you should we have to fight, for something that is rightfully yours.

Why don't they just hand over the keys, to unlock all those frozen doors?

What kind of a country do we live in, that sees people's trust and faith on the wane?

This country seems to hang on to its justice, unless it has something to gain.

What kind of country do we live in, when the voice of the ordinary person is the last to be heard.

And what chance do you stand against the police, with their lies already carefully prepared.

I'll tell you what kind of country we live in, one where deceit and corruption is rife.

A country where you can get off scot free, for causing the loss of a football fan's life.

Don't Waste Your Breath

Don't waste your valuable breath shouting for help, you may
as well save your air.
Some coppers walked by and ignored people's cries; they just
didn't seem to care.
Some fans stood dead, bolt upright, and other fans thought
their time had come.
People packed together so tight they couldn't move a muscle,
only eye contact was possible for some.
One fan who thought his life was over counted down from 60,
not really knowing why.
He decided to countdown the last minute of his life, he felt it
was soon his turn to die.
How should you use the last of your breath, you may as well
use it for saying a prayer.
Shouting for help seemed such a waste, because some
coppers just didn't seem to care.

Frozen Scars

Let's crack the truth wide open, in these early days of the winter woes.
I'm tired of the victims always losing out to all the villains and the foes.
Let's split straight through all the lies, let's just see what there is to find.
Let's see who got away with what, unravel the red tape, let it all unwind.
This morning the weather was freezing, windscreens all wore frozen scars.
But the sun soon melted that ice away, as daylight replaced the stars.
This city has unfairly carried a burden, of which we long deserve to be free.
That burden being one of injustice, still there for the whole world to see.
We will put the names of all the liars in lights, lights that will forever glow.
This winter may be a harsh one, but time will always melt away the snow.

No Need For Dreams

When you awake from your sleep, a different sort of world you must find.
So different from this world, that all those years ago you had to leave behind.
When you awake from your sleep, and open your eyes and look around.
Love and happiness you must see everywhere, no sorrow to be found.
This world I find myself in now, it can be so heartless and it can be so cruel.
I look around and I see conflict, there's always an ongoing battle or duel.
I try to dream those problems away, escaping reality are what dreams are for.
But I imagine once in heaven, there would be no reason to dream anymore.
So for all the Hillsborough victims, there's no need to dream this or any other night.
Because every day they wake up, they must wake up to a beautiful sight.

This Tunnel

I'm in this tunnel, this long, long tunnel and it's as dark as it can be.
I've been in this tunnel for such a long time, yet any light I'm still to see.
I'm in this tunnel, this depressing tunnel, a tunnel as black as ink.
There have been times in this tunnel when to new depths I've had to sink.

I've been in this tomb of a tunnel for over 20 years and I know other people are around.
Yet sometimes I just choose to ignore them but other times I'm so desperate to be found.
I'm stuck in this tunnel, this never ending tunnel, where there's no difference between day and night.
And all the time I've spent in this tunnel all I've asked for is just a ray of light.

There have been periods that I've felt so low I've been unable to function or cope.
And deep in thought I've often wondered has all the light gone out on hope?
Nearly 22 years in this tunnel, you could say I'm getting used to being alone.
So will I be rescued from this tunnel, or this tunnel will I finally call home?

No Debate

Use it to start a fire with, watch it melt within the flame.
Hide it under other newspapers, so nobody will see its
name.
Chuck it in to the River Mersey watch those scouse waves
take it below.
Tell everyone about the boycott, so more strength we
have to show.
Deny all things Mackenzie; never forgive him for what he
did.
Just like that picture shows this rag belongs down the grid.
Challenge any scouser you see reading it, some people you
may need to educate.
Tell them The Scum should never see the light of day in
Liverpool of that there's no debate.

21 Years of Freedom

21 years of freedom and you were safe in the knowledge for a while.
That you would never face any punishment, even before you stood any trial.
21 years of freedom, and never in any danger of being anything but free.
21 years of freedom, this British justice system just doesn't seem fair to me.
21 years of freedom, and most of them spent living leisurely on the coast.
You've never had to miss those little things in life and those little things you can miss the most.
Those mistakes you made you never paid for, your uniform saw you through.
You've lived your life a free man, though our calls for justice grew and grew.
21 years of freedom, happily watching your family and love ones grow.
21 years of gross injustice more like it, but just how I'll never ever know.

Dog Handlers Needed

Put away those fire engines and your ambulances we don't need.
Dog handlers is what we want, let's make those fuckers bleed.
We're just worthless footy fans in your eyes, nothing but scouse scum.
And no doubt we'll take all the blame, for what you lot have done.

Those fire engines had the gear to cut through those fences of steel.
But the police didn't want them early on, they made no such appeal.
Crowd safety was never an issue, just a case of keeping them under control.
Every Liverpool fan a potential hooligan and most of them on the dole.

That's how the police mostly saw us, in the Thatcher years of Tory rule.
Every copper was seen to be brave and most scousers seen to be cruel.
Liverpool fans running on to the pitch I think just meant one thing to the law.
And that was a pitch invasion had begun, and that's why the dog handlers were called for.

The Search

We've searched for the truth in this land and we've searched for it across the sea.
Why would they want to hide the truth from us, it just doesn't seem right to me.
We've searched for justice within this Isle; we've also searched beyond this shore.
Why have they made us do this for so long, is this not a fair world anymore?
We've searched in all the right places, a search that's been thorough, high and wide.
But the powers that be are crafty, and they have dark places for the truth to hide.
They shut doors in people's faces; they wrap lies up in red tape, home and abroad.
But we'll get those answers we want in the end, of that all the liars can be assured.
Join in this search for the truth, give a hand to lift and turn every last heavy stone.
Show everyone the strength of our fight, and show them that we will never fight alone.

Emotions

It's taken years of hard work and dedication; it's been a long slog made without fear.
It's taken over 21 years to get people to listen, to make our message loud and clear.
But I'm an older person now, I'm more patient, I suppose I've just learnt how to wait.
I've grown to know what it means to forgive, but I still understand what it means to hate.
I still know what it means to feel anger and I still know what it means to feel hurt.
I'll never forgive certain people for their lies, and for their newspaper printing dirt.
I still shed tears when I try to imagine, what it must have been like in other people's shoes.
I think of the agony faced by a Father seeing his daughters, then the heartache of having to choose.
Hillsborough has opened up many of my emotions, emotions that might have remained dormant who knows.
Emotions that can wear down your heart and mind, but emotions that you just can't simply shut down and close.

Early Doors

We still live in a country of relative free speech, so I suppose
then that it's only fair.
But Irvine Patnick, MP for Hallam spoke about Hillsborough,
as if he was actually there.
His comments though hurtful and wrong were widely used,
as an MP he probably had more clout.
It didn't seem to matter that much, that he didn't have a clue
what he was talking about.
So Irvine Patnick's comments set the wheels of propaganda
and lies quickly into motion.
More big hitters soon climbed on board and mixed their lies
into the poisonous potion.
Why didn't people sit back and wait, give themselves time to
think, to ponder and reflect?
Were they that desperate to apportion the blame, the focus
and attention elsewhere to deflect?
Douglas Hurd in the House of Commons also inferred some
wrongful comments early doors.
He couldn't back up those comments though, and didn't
seem to mind what distress he may cause.
Ignorance lives on today through the likes of Jeremy Hunt,
and he continues that political trend.
As some Tories seem intent on ignoring the facts over
Hillsborough, when will this ever end?

Faces

I'm looking through a sea of faces, though I'm only trying to pick out three
As long as I see thousands of faces then there's still some hope for me.
Hope to see the ones that I love, to see that they are safe and sound.
As I wait where we'd arranged to meet by a corner shop close to the ground.
Those thousands of faces soon became hundreds, if only there was something I could do.
Has God even heard my frantic prayers yet, or am I the last one in the queue?
Those hundreds of faces then become just dozens, as the crowd starts to thin out.
Then soon there are even less people around, and there are not many faces about.
The crowds are now disappearing, and I grow wary to what this may mean.
As those three faces that I long to see so much, are still nowhere to be seen.

Rain

Battle hardened, but with time I also feel sometimes battle scarred.
I read the poignant words written on a rain drenched memorial card.
A card signed with loving kisses, which have started to 'run' in the rain.
If only those winter elements could simply wash away our pain.
Battle weary, but I know there's still much more to be said and done.
We have to carry on fighting the cause, until that fight is finally won.
Been down but never out, we've got up many times from our knees.
As I take heart from that card, which begins to dry off in the breeze.

Time

The years suddenly pass by; they stack up quickly one by one.
21 years passed already, I wonder where they've all gone.
And in all those 21 years, flickered brightly has that flame.
And because of what happened that day, some people have never been the same.
The years rack up, people get older and memories begin to fade.
The children today need to know about those mistakes that were made.
Our city has celebrated many highs, and some people say that we wallow in the lows.
But to me we just are unique; it's something in our blood that flows.
The years suddenly fly by and seem to pass by at breakneck speed.
They also say time is a healer, dry your eyes and take all of it that you need.
But this year is another year that I haven't rid of all my tears just yet.
In time maybe I will start to forgive, but at no time will I ever start to forget.

Liar's Knife

You cut in deep with your liar's knife, causing us no end of
distress and pain.
You rubbished our fans you rubbished our city, while our
tears still fell like rain.
You had an agenda to keep, you had backs to cover, you
worked closely to get it right.
You left no stone unturned to dish out the blame, while
dreaming up alibis watertight.
You cut in deep with your poisonous knife; you kept cutting
until you bled us dry.
Does your conscience ever bother you now, do you ever
think back and ask yourself why?
Do you ever regret the harm that you did to us while you
held that knife in your hand?
Have you ever given our feelings a second thought, have
you ever tried to understand?
You must feel a twinge of guilt and remorse in those
moments when you're left alone.
If not, can you please tell me what it's like to have a heart
that's made out of stone?

The Nightmare of Hillsborough

A tear drop drips from your eye, and onto your pillow it falls.
You eventually drift into sleep, although another restless night calls.
You awaken in the night, your brow soaked in beads of sweat.
You were once fed a Hillsborough nightmare, one you've never been able to forget.
You long to switch off your mind, to taste the freedom of sanity once more.
You've been down many a dark avenue desperately searching for a cure.
But some people don't realise that you're ill and just cruelly turn their back.
These people just see a defeated person, but it's understanding that they lack.
And in your head you carry around with you a heavy stone of grief.
It weighs you down and it wears you down, no respite however brief.
This torture follows you around in the form of your own personal Hillsborough Hell.
If only sleep could offer you an escape, but your visions you still cannot quell.
A tear drop drips from your eye, and it won't be the last tear that you shed.
The nightmare of Hillsborough you wake up to, as well as take to your bed.

The 'Truth'

The 'Truth', you splashed out on that disgusting front page.

Headlines with no substance written to grab centre stage.

Endless reasons we have why it's a rag we still all despise.

Three points you highlighted nothing but a pack of dirty lies.

Robbed from the injured you said another falsehood not fact.

Unfounded gutter trash, because the government you backed.

The boycott in our glorious city remains as strong to this day.

Hatred is what we feel for you, and it will always be that way.

Hillsborough Park Memorial Garden.

For 21 Years

An injustice was done right on our doorstep, our city then left to pay the price.
21 years of heartache, caused by a justice system with a heart as cold as ice.
They knew the score, they knew the truth, but they set their stall out right from the start.
They let the scousers carry the burden, that would eventually weigh down many a broken heart.

We've held marches, we've flown banners and the Kop's mosaic has pleaded for the truth.
You've lied, we all know that you've lied, so you've robbed this city of our justice and our proof.
You stole what's rightfully ours, you owe us, and now it's about time that you paid us back.
Don't you think that we've all suffered enough, as this city seemed under constant attack.

Attacked by government officials, and by senior police officers with their carefully worded alibis.
Attacked and accused by a rag of a newspaper, that hurt us with their dirty, foul lies.
For 21 years we've suffered this hurt, with a dignity that this city can truly be proud.
As the people in this city are a little different, we tend to stand out from the crowd

For 21 years, I don't suppose much time for those families has ever passed them by.
When they've thought to themselves and asked the questions just how and just why?
Why still no justice, why not all the answers and why do you still make us shed more tears?
So don't you think it's time to clean now, after all, you've made us all wait for 21 long years?

Still Believe

When you see an injustice of that scale, and read so many lies of that kind.
It's very hard for me to forgive, and put it all to the back of my mind.
When I see a copy of the Sun, it reminds me what lies it told about our brave fans.
That's why today I still believe in justice, and why I still support boycotts and bans.

Last year the world's media cries for justice must have been at an all time high.
Will the media care as much this year, or will Hillsborough just pass them by?
Yes, as an anniversary 20 years was a special time, but it shouldn't mean things have reached their peak.
After all, we are now another year on, yet justice and the truth we still seek.

I still believe in wearing my justice scarf and in wearing my 'HJC' badges with pride.
I still believe in searching for the truth, until the truth has got no place to hide.
I still believe a '6 Minute Chant' for justice, should last exactly that, 6 minutes long.
Because at this time of year especially, that chant means more to me than the words to any other song.

The Myths of Hillsborough Dispelled

Mythical can mean something fabled, fabricated, fanciful, unreal or untrue.
Most people can distinguish a myth from fact; it's not really that hard to do.
A myth can normally be dispelled once hard evidence puts it under threat.
A myth becomes nothing more than a piece of pretence, once the truth is finally met.
Myths surround the Hillsborough disaster, myths that inexplicably live on.
Myths supported only by outdated lies, lies all dispelled long ago one by one.
The disaster unfolded before Television cameras and was recorded on CCTV.
Yet people still cling to the myths, why don't they believe what their eyes can see.
Plenty of life remain in these Hillsborough myths; it's remarkable how they're still sustained.
Why don't people just acknowledge the Taylor report and all the facts that it contained?

Prisoners

There were unnecessary bars and fences at Hillsborough as that was the norm at the time.
And nobody has ever been put behind bars because of Hillsborough, because nobody has paid for their crime.
But barriers and bars can take on many forms, and some people are behind them right now.
An innocent person can only taste as much freedom that a dominant, detached mind will allow.

'Prison bars' can exist outside the walls of a prison; they are not confined to the inside of a cell.
Such bars can be found in just about all walks of life, each one with its own sad story to tell.
The Hillsborough disaster has caused so many people to suffer, these people too are prisoners of a kind.
Sometimes trapped forever to a sentence of pain and self destruction, due to an ever dissolving mind.

The condition these people suffer with can come with a stigma, it can be overlooked and misunderstood.
The prison bars that surround these innocent victims, they often find will surround them for good.
People suffered from mental health illness because of Hillsborough, and still do so to this very day.
No blame or guilt to be burdened with, yet a heavy and sometimes ultimate price some people continue to pay.

Eeny,Meeny,Miny Moe

Eeny,meeny,miny moe.
Catch a copper then let him go.
Watch him walk free from court.
Admire the cottage that his pension bought.

Eeny,meeny,miny moe.
Tell a lie then watch it grow.
I'll boycott that newspaper for evermore.
For the lies it told, that it was fed by the law.

Eeny,meeny,miny moe.
Listen to that shite on a U.S radio show.
He's been proved to be wrong and a liar so many times.
Doesn't Cohen understand that coppers do commit crimes?

Eeny, meeny, miny moe.
Check out the sick abuse, sung by the lowest of the low.
Can't these thick idiots actually get it into their brain
That 96 innocent people actually died in their name?

Eeny,meeny,miny moe.
Light a candle, and then watch it glow.
Watch it glow forever in its eternal case.
While we continue our fight, no matter what barriers we face.

'Stolen' Witness

Just how do you steal a witness that seems such a strange
and odd thing to say?
But that's what happened to 2 tapes of CCTV footage that
somehow went astray.
Why do you treat us all like fools, just how stupid and naive
do we think we all are?
Every lie you've told we've seen through, though each one
of them has left a scar.

So what really happened to those tapes of footage, you took
a light to them I guess.
Then you made up your ridiculous story, and with a straight
face then fed it to the press.
'2 CCTV tapes have been stolen' you revealed, but nothing
important on them you said.
Nobody man enough to accept responsibility, so did you all
turned to lies instead?

I wonder what those tapes would have shown and why they
weren't under lock and key.
So were they ever 'stolen' at all or were they quietly
removed by the powers that be?
Somehow vital evidence disappeared, right under the South
Yorkshire Police force's nose.
A 'crime' with no apparent rhyme or reason, that's because
it didn't really exist I suppose.

Goodnight

I'm writing this at almost midnight, though I thought I had
nothing else to say.
But these few words just came into my head, just sort of
come my way.
Just want to say you'll always be remembered, your flame
will always burn bright.
And before this day is through, I just wanted to say to you all
'Goodnight'
And tomorrow belongs to you, in the heart of this great city
you'll truly belong.
Tomorrow tears will flow for you at Anfield, with every prayer
and with every song.
But before that day soon arrives, and before I now switch
out the light.
I just wanted to say to you again, 'God bless you all and
goodnight'.

Silk Purse
(The West Midlands Police)

Officers in smart expensive Armani suits, sent to Merseyside with a 'job to do'
Clothing allowances given to look the part, for overtime, no need to form a queue.
Softly softly approach, but a bit of subtle pressure sustained here and there.
First name terms, and ultra friendly persona, but deep down did they really care?
A high ranking copper with a major role to play, but he himself was not so clean.
An investigator himself being investigated, now what's that supposed to mean?
The West Midlands Police investigating 'Hillsborough' a silk purse their clever disguise
They worked their 'magic' on many, but many others could see through their lies.

Moving Waters

A lot of water has passed under the bridge since then, I've watched most of it ebb and flow
Because just like a tide under the power of the moon, it just won't let me go.
I've dealt with many things in my life and time seems to melt most things away.
But Hillsborough has its feet firmly under the table, and would like to stay another day.
And stay it will until we get the truth, until we squeeze out every last single drop.
Until that day we'll continue to shout for justice, from the steps of the mighty Kop.
And as the years hang on to this tragedy, and on other people's lives it still takes its toll.
It just gives me more reason to carry on fighting, until we finally reach our justice goal.
So I'll keep on watching those moving waters, looking out for every ripple that they make.
And if it starts to take its toll on me, well that's just a chance that I'm willing to take.

Rolling The Ball

This one is for you Bernard Ingham, it was you who started
rolling the ball.
You acted very quickly to ensure that the Police didn't take
any blame at all.
This one is for you Bernard Ingham, are you proud that you
cast the first stone?
You needlessly caused so much damage before waiting for
the truth to be known.

So just what did you hear on that day, to tell the world what
you 'learnt on the spot'?
Did you believe the lies Duckenfield and Wright were they
the only stories that you got?
So you went and told your beloved Sun, that the disaster
was caused by 'a tanked up mob'
That rag dressed up the rest, including stories of those
heartless scousers on the rob.

This was in the day before the term 'black art of spin' was
used, but I think it's fair to say.
That in April 1989 you had your own agenda, and that you
were clearly 'spinning' away.
And just like Tories old and new with that same agenda,
you've always stood by what you said.
This city has still not recovered Mr Ingham, from all those
lies that you helped to spread.

26 Years On Average

They say it takes 26 years on average, to put a miscarriage of justice right.
Let's hope we get ours before that, people deserve it for their dedication and fight.
26 years, an awful lot of doors must get slammed in decent people's face.
If only there was some way to stop this, because 26 years seems a disgrace.
26 years to right something, they must have an army of people to stand in the way.
How long would it take to achieve the truth, if people didn't fight for it every day?
The answer to that is probably 'never' just how certain people would like it to be.
Then those old dusty old boxes of files would be forgotten, forever under lock and key.
For within those files lies the truth, hidden away on some distant Parliamentary shelves
But will we see each word they hold, or will they keep something back for themselves?

One Minute...

One minute you could all hear the songs, just like it was meant to be.
But those songs got quieter and quieter as the clock ticked towards 3.
A beautiful spring day for football, an eagerly awaited Cup semi final tie.
But why did anyone have to suffer, why did so many people have to die?

As 3 o' clock got closer, the noise levels from the crowd gradually rose.
Just like it does at every other football match, you know just how it goes.
But this was no ordinary football match, the police were losing control.
A wrong decision was about to be made, by a man not fit for his role.

And so the football match started, but not all eyes were following the play.
Crucial mistakes were being made by the police, cries for help were being turned away.
The singing from the Liverpool fans had now almost come to a complete stop.
But those songs would probably still be heard, if Liverpool fans had been given the Hillsborough Kop.

And so when the children open their history books in many years to come.
They will learn of exactly just what happened that day, beneath the April sun.
They will wonder why at a football match, that 96 innocent people had to fall.
As even when every question has been answered, it'll still make no sense at all.

Better Days

Think back to April 1989, when that terrible tragedy sadly took place.
Think back and remember that senior policeman, more interested in saving face.
Remember the Sun newspaper accusing Liverpool fans, with all their guns full blaze.
I think it's fair to say that the truth in this country, had seen much better days.

Remember it came to light, that the police had lied in their statements and notes.
Do you recall a press officer blaming 'a tanked up mob' for the tragedy, no doubt seeking Tory votes.
There were deals being done out of court, so nobody would pay for the error of their ways.
So I think it's fair to say that justice in this country had seen much better days.

So here we are now in Liverpool, Hillsborough may be 21 years down the line.
But we're still fighting for justice and the truth, and it looks like we've still got a mountain to climb.
Because some people will hang on to the words of Hunt and Hawker, and the issues that they incorrectly raise.
So I'll say it once again that the truth in this country, has seen much better days.

Rapids

Once a blue sky is above you, you can never take it away.
You cannot stop the sun from shining, once it's a sunny day.
You'll never stop the waves of the ocean, once they start to roll.
Those things will always happen, because they are beyond our control.
Nobody can prevent the moon, from ever rising each night in the sky.
And nobody will stop us from getting to the bottom, of each and every lie.
You could never stop the rapids, once those rapids are in full flow.
And you'll never stop our fight for the truth, because we never intend to let go.

Hard Time

Please don't give me a hard time, at least just let me have
my say.
Don't let the years cloud the issue; don't let them stand in
the way.
21 years of injustice and cover-ups woven under a
corruption spell.
Just look into many of our eyes as they have their own story
to tell.
This fight could have been won 10 times over, but they insist
on holding the truth back.
But we will keep on applying the pressure, until finally the
right people crack.
If you're young and don't understand about Hillsborough,
then give education a try.
Learn about all the lies that we were told and how we were
hung out to dry.
Don't give anybody a hard time fighting for justice, don't
belittle all what they do.
These people are actually fighting your corner so one day a
'Hillsborough 'wont happen to you.

The Last Plinther

Emma Burns stood alone on the 4th Plinth high up in
London's Trafalgar Square.
Her 96 red balloons in bunches all set to be released into
the cold October air.
She spoke fondly of the Hillsborough victims; she spoke of
them in the name of art.
Plinther 2,400 was London's final plinther, and she took
everyone to her heart.
Emma was honoured an extra 3 minutes to read out all the
names of the Hillsborough dead.
She was surrounded by her justice placards and banners
carved out in Liverpool red.
And the crowds below her sang 'You'll Never Walk Alone' as
she cut the last balloon free.
Congratulations to the final plinther, the most meaningful
plinther that London got to see.

A Queue Without Noise

I've queued up countless times outside Anfield, back in the
days when you could pay at the gate.
Sometimes before you reached the Kop turnstile, it could be
a two or three hour wait.
I remember starting to feel all tense and nervous, as my turn
to get into the ground drew near.
All the fans in the queue felt the same way, as getting locked
out was the Kopites biggest fear.

A different sort of queue once developed outside Anfield, it
was still massive and went back a very long way.
But this queue was eerie in its silence; I think people in it
just couldn't find the right words to say.
And as you slowly approached the Kop, there were no hats,
scarves or badges that you could buy.
People's heads were all bowed in sorrow and a tangle of
different emotions were all running high.

As that huge queue of people silently moved along, they
saw a flag that was flying at half mast.
A flag which flew at 'flagpole corner,' a meeting place with a
link to our long and glorious past.
But on that day our glorious past meant nothing to me, I just
didn't seem to care.
I remember just searching my head for reasons and
answers', but not being able to find any there.

As my turn nearly came to enter the Kop, an overpowering
sense of the occasion seemed to take over me.
My old Liverpool scarf was about to be given a new home,
but why should this have to be?
So then my wait was over, and with some reluctance I finally
entered our famous old ground.
While thousands more still stood in that queue behind me,
and yet there still was hardly a sound.

Turn It Loose

You've known the truth for long enough now; it's time that
you turned it loose.
A justice system that protects the guilty parties, please tell
me what's the use?
Look after the innocent ones, fight for the bereaved families,
surely that's the only thing to do.
Let the truth now be known, no more need to fight for it, I
think our time is now due.

You've reopened the files only due to our pressure, so don't
pretend that you've done us a good turn.
I'm sure you'd like to see all those files rot, leave nothing
new for us to discover or to learn.
Then you could finally draw a line under all the deceit, and
kiss goodbye to the whole sorry affair.
You've hidden the facts from us for so long now, so please
don't pretend that you now care.

And will there ever be a fresh enquiry; I don't think that will
ever be the case.
So even when we uncover the truth, nobody will have a
prosecution to face.
As justice gets harder to achieve over the years, people get
older, people get ill and people die.
The truth indeed we may discover, but justice for the 96 I
fear has now sadly passed us by.

Credit Where Credit Is Due

A police officer described his colleagues at Hillsborough as
'headless chickens' not knowing what to do.
But some officers did act on their own initiative as the senior
officers didn't seem to have a clue.
Some junior officers tried to relieve the pressure at the back of
the tunnel, they did this off their own back.
These cops realised the gravity of the situation, they understood
that nobody was under attack.
Roger Greenwood, the Ground Commander ran on the pitch
without instruction, to alert the ref to call the game to a halt.
He's another example that not every police officer at
Hillsborough was to blame or was at fault.
We'll always remember those coppers at Hillsborough who *were*
at fault, who were a disgrace to their uniform in every way.
But some officers did their best and carried out their duties, and
I should have acknowledged that before today.

Peter Beardsley's Shot

Peter Beardsley hit the Forest crossbar, just about 4 minutes into the game.
Thank God there was no early goal to celebrate down at the Leppings Lane.
Beardsley's shot had beaten the Forest keeper, there was nothing he could do.
But thank God that Peter Beardsley's shot wasn't lower by an inch or two.
Beardsley came so close to scoring, but thank God we didn't go a goal ahead.
Thank God that the game stayed at 0-0 and not 1-0 to the team in all red.
Thank God Beardsley's shot hit the bar and nobody scored from a rebound.
Had Liverpool scored a goal then, there would have further chaos at one side of the ground.
Beardsley's shot had goal written all over it, but thankfully it never hit the net.
As nobody deserves to score such a 'goal' that he would forever live to regret.

'The Classic Smear'

MacKenzie was faced with a dilemma; he didn't know what headline he would choose.
'YOU SCUM' was one option he considered, 'THE TRUTH' was the other he might use.
Most staff in his office shuddered at these words, but MacKenzie was a one man band.
Unquestioned he would publish one of these vile headlines, to be read all over the land.
Everyone knew of the backlash using such words, they knew it would cause an outrage.
But unnerved MacKenzie went ahead, 'THE TRUTH' he chose to headline the front page.
And so he made his decision, a decision made without conscience and made without fear.
In the book 'Stick It Up Your Punter' they accused MacKenzie of producing 'the classic smear'

A Survivor?

I'm not one of the '96 'as all of me didn't die that day.
But a big part of me did; now life just gets in the way.
They say that I was lucky, but that word doesn't seem to fit the bill.
'Lucky' to suffer for 20 years, 'lucky' to suffer nightmares still.
I *did* come home that day, the day I saw people turn blue.
But to my loved ones I'm saying sorry, because I can't see this agony through.
I didn't die that day, for me they put a separate day aside.
Hillsborough didn't take me that day, but it still made sure that I died.

Shame

Shame about all that police paper work, all discarded,
ignored and torn.
It could have been used in a court of law, under an oath
truthfully sworn.
When I think of those officers match day notes, I think of the
sound of paper being ripped.
Shame then for all those honest coppers, now ordered to
read from a different script.
Shame that those senior officers felt that their police force
was above the law.
Shame they just couldn't accept responsibility, hold their
hands up and face the score.
If only those accounts and notes that were written were left
untouched, unchanged and intact.
They would have told the world a different story, which
included every nailed on fact.
Shame then all this didn't happen, and all that vital evidence
allowed to be dismissed.
I thought we were above that sort of corruption in this
country, but now I know such things exist.

The Strongest Boycott

I've just been to the local Newsagents wearing my HJC scarf
to keep me warm.
As it was another cold winter's night, with a slight frost
already starting to form.
I found that as I went into the shop which was about to close
up for the day.
The owner was tying up unsold copies of The Sun, and this
is what he had to say.
He told me that he only stocked that rag because of some
contractual clause.
And that he actually put people off buying it and would
explain our Justice cause.
Not that many people tried to buy it anyway he said, which
was music to my ears.
And that's the way it's always been he went on, and always
will be for many years.
As nobody in these parts will ever forgive that paper, not for
the day it cruelly lied.
The day ends up like every other day in his shop, with
copies of the scum all bundled up and tied.

Christmas Kiss

Tears at this time of year can be expected to more freely and sadly flow.
As Christmas brings out people's emotions, and can leave them feeling low.
So when you shed a tear this Christmas for your loved ones that you still sorely miss.
Think of them in a better place, because heaven is a much better place than this.

When you hear a bell ring at Christmas they say an angel always springs to mind.
An angel can mean a different thing to different people, and there must be many a different kind.
So when I hear a bell ring this Christmas I'll think of 96 angels close to home.
These are our very own special angels who we promised would never walk alone.

This Christmas will just be like every other one, all 21 that have gone before.
We will remember all the friends that we lost, in our hearts a place we'll store.
When you give out all your Christmas kisses this year, save one, it's something you won't regret.
And blow that kiss all the way to heaven, to show the 96 that you'll never forget.

The House That Jack Built

This is the house that Jack built, a house where lies can be safely stored.
This is the house that Jack built, where the justice system lives all sadly flawed.
This is the house that Jack built, a house where many dark secrets are kept.
This is the house that Jack built, where lots of guilty people have soundly slept.

This is the house that Jack built, with its windows all disguised and painted black.
This is the house that Jack built, where dreams were stolen and never given back.
This is the house that Jack built, a house born and raised from blood red bricks.
This is the house that Jack built, where people conjure up all their dirty tricks.

This is the house that Jack built, where in the corrupted corridors the people deal.
This is the house that Jack built, a house with so much it won't give up or reveal.
This is the house that Jack built, its foundations all rotten, each and every stone.
This is the house that Jack built, what sort of people would want to call this home?

This is the house that Jack built, with its floors of polished marble, a visitor's treat.
This is the house that Jack built; within its walls the chosen few can hide their deceit.
This is the house that Jack built, where safety and freedom for liars is guaranteed.
This is the house that Jack built, where people live and die but never seem to bleed.

That was the house that Jack built, where our heartless enemies all live under one roof.
But the house that Jack built won't stand forever; we'll bring it down one day with the truth.

Hillsborough Hell

How are you doing as a survivor, since that day how has your life been?
How many Doctors have you visited, how many more psychiatrists still to be seen?
Have they sorted your mind out yet, have they got to the bottom of your ills?
And since you lost your job a long time ago, who pays your medical bills?
I believe you've never been to the match again, as it would be too much for you to bear.
Football was once the love of your life, but now you hardly give it a care.
I'm so happy that you're a survivor, but it seems to have come at quite a cost.
I imagine you must often think about all the things in life that you've lost.
You escaped with your life from Hillsborough, but now you just exist inside your shell.
As you're just a shadow of the person you once were, since you survived your Hillsborough hell.

And So It Goes On

And so it goes on, the list of ignorant people seems to grow and grow.

People are still causing upset and damage, probably more than they'll ever know.

The facts have been long established over Hillsborough, there's no excuse not to know the score.

A little research would soon reveal the truth, and isn't that research is for?

But a writer for the Boston Globe decided to take the lazy journalistic route.

He put Hillsborough down to 'a riot' and then decided to further put in the boot.

He accused Liverpool fans as still 'agonising' about something that happened a long time ago.

Does he expect us to put a cap on grief, with no more respect or sorrow to show?

So Alex Beam, an apology to all the people of Liverpool I think from you is now due.

Because our City is now getting sick and tired at the ignorance of people like you.

Heartless

'But it was 21 years ago' you said about Hillsborough, yes it was, but so what?
There should never be a time limit on achieving the truth and justice, is that true or not?
Or should we forget all about justice as time goes on, is that what you want us to believe?
You've opened up old wounds with your hurtful comments, don't you understand what it means to grieve?
People like you always puzzle me; your ignorance and insensitivity seem to know no bounds.
You make a case that simply defies the truth; you make blatant accusations without any grounds.
You admit that you still stand by your opinion, but you don't have a shred of evidence to back up your claim.
Because the facts are stacked up against you Mr Hawker, so you should hang your head in shame.
'But it was 21 years ago' you said about Hillsborough, you ought to stand before the bereaved and explain just what you mean.
But you're the sort of person that seems above doing that, because you're just an arrogant and heartless person it would seem.

HILLSBOROUGH

H... stands for '**HOPE FOR JUSTICE**', to which we all still hold in our heart.

I... stands for that '**INJUSTICE**', clearly put in place right from the start.

L... stands for '**LORD JUSTICE TAYLOR**', he dissolved our fans from any blame.

L... stands for '**LEPPINGS LANE**', an unfit terrace to stage such a game.

S... stands for the '**SUN**' newspaper, the ultimate in the British gutter press.

B... stands for '**BROKEN HEARTS**', all caused through grief, pain and distress.

O... stands for '**OPEN THAT GATE**', an order made by Duckenfield about Gate 'C'

R... stands for '**REFEREE**' Ray Lewis, who halted the game at 6 minutes past 3.

O... stands for '**ON RUSHING SUPPORTERS**', all existing cctv footage disproves this claim.

U... stands for '**UNEVEN DISTRIBUTION OF FANS**', for which the police were clearly to blame.

G... stands for '**GROUNDS FOR CONCERN**', safety fears over Hillsborough had already been shared.

H... stands for the '**HOME SECRETARY**', a conservative liar whose name was Douglas Hurd.

Ticketless Fans

Another Hillsborough myth that needs addressing another lie that needs putting to bed.

Another false accusation made by a Policeman, without any evidence not a single shred.

"500 plus'" ticketless fans were "hell bent" on getting in, it was reported on the ITV News.

A figure Paul Middup must have just plucked out of the air with nothing to back up his views.

There will always be some ticketless football fans that turn up at big matches of this type.

It doesn't mean that they are "hell bent" on getting in, it was just more anti fan PR hype.

The Taylor Report states there was no truth to the allegations that ticketless fans were partly to blame.

So to the list of people that created a Hillsborough myth, we can safely add another name.

Hello The People of Sheffield

Hello the people of Sheffield would you like to talk about exactly what happened that day.

As its apparent some of you still believe that the Liverpool fans were to blame in some way.

I don't blame you for defending your city and for defending your police force to the hilt.

But you have to accept reality that the Liverpool fans have never needed to feel any guilt.

Hello the people of Sheffield just sit down for a moment with a bit more of an open mind.

Try to think beyond the loyalties of your hometown, and you'll be surprised at what you'll find.

I fully understand why you would stand by your city; most people would do exactly the same.

But on this occasion you have to hold your hands up and admit Liverpool fans were not to blame.

The proof of our innocence is all out there, it's official, it's all written clearly in black and white.

Read the Taylor Report if you still doubt me and you'll soon realise that what I'm saying is right.

Midnight

You won't be forgotten at midnight as the bells for New Year peel.
We'll raise a glass to you all to let you know how we feel.
You won't be alone at midnight, as we see the New Year in.
You won't be far from our hearts, as all the celebrations begin.
We'll remember you at midnight as we say farewell this old decade.
10 more years of fight behind us, every effort is still being made.
So as we welcome the New Year in, we'll raise a glass high in the air.
To show that you'll always be remembered and that we'll always care.

Post - Traumatic Stress Disorder (PTSD)

Post-traumatic stress disorder, it affects so many people you will find.
It can destroy or take over your life; it can slowly eat away at your aching mind.
Some people it can haunt forever some come out unscathed on the other side.
Some sufferers try to run away from it, while some try and find a place to hide.

PTSD sufferers sometimes feel that their burden can be just too heavy a load.
Sometimes that weight on their shoulders can mean only the end of the road.
Some people will learn to live with the struggle, though they struggle in every way.
While others sadly decide that they just can't suffer PTSD, for yet another day.

PTSD can cause vivid flashbacks, nightmares and the suppression of pent up tears.
PTSD sufferers have been known to suffer in silence, and to suffer alone for years.
Many people lose their faith in those around them; their sense of trust may be lost.
PTSD can turn you inside out, and loved ones might be left alone to count the cost.

Post-Traumatic Stress Disorder is sometimes described as a 'cycle of guilt and shame'
Sufferers will sometimes ignore guilty parties and choose instead to shoulder the blame.
People took their own lives due to PTSD after Hillsborough, it tore countless others apart.
Marriages failed, lives were ruined, because some people found it impossible to make a fresh start.

To Sum Up

We didn't cause 'a riot' and we didn't steal from the dead.
We didn't 'kill our own' despite what Brian Clough said.
We didn't piss on 'brave cops' and we didn't beat up a P.C
We were not 'a tanked up mob' whatever that's meant to be.
Hillsborough wasn't caused by 'ticketless fans' that turned up drunk and late.
And we didn't force our way in, it was Duckenfield who opened that gate.
So every myth accounted for, we've put right every wrong call.
Every lie been told about us, we've disproved them one and all.

'Justice For All'

One day I hope we see a world, where there's no need to fight for Justice at all.

Fair play should be the norm and no more backs should be strapped to the wall.

I'd like to see a world where people who hurt others have to pay for that hurt.

I'd like to see a world where it's not so easy to wash your hands free of any dirt.

One day I'd like to see a world where a lie, is a lie is a lie.

Every person should be accountable for their actions even if their position is high.

So I'd like to finish this book off, with these final few words if I may.

I hope to see the overused plea 'Justice for All' be made redundant one day.

 The Nightmare of Hillsborough

15/04/1989

Justice For All

Acknowledgements/Contacts

Thanks to Rachel King for kindly writing the foreword to this book and to LFC.TV: www.Liverpoolfctv.com for their ongoing support.

Mental Health Reg Charity Imagine:
www.imaginementalhealth.org.uk

HJC (Hillsborough Justice Campaign):
Email: hjcshop@tiscali.co.uk

HFSG (Hillsborough Family Support Group):
www.hfsg.co.uk

Hope for Hillsborough: www.hopeforhillsborough.org

Hillsborough Football Disaster Contents & Consequences: www.hfdinfo.com

News From Nowhere
(Independent book shop in Bold St. Liverpool)

Other Hillsborough Poetry Books Available

**HILLSBOROUGH 20 YEARS ON (Compilation)
ISBN: 9781 906823 153**

**JUSTICE CALL (Mike Bartram)
ISBN: 9781 906823 283**

The above publications can be ordered at any major book retailer or are available online through Countyvise, Amazon, eBay, HJC shop, HFSG etc.

For more Hillsborough poetry: www.Redandwhitekop.com

This book was co-funded between the HJC and myself. Many thanks to Gerry, Sheila, Steve, Kenny and all at the HJC for their continued help and financial support

Once again many thanks to all at Countyvise:
www.countyvise.co.uk

Mike Bartram (dandy.77@hotmail.co.uk)